welcome

You are about to take a wonderful journey, and I am so excited for you. The fact that you have this journal tells me that you, through the leading of the Holy Spirit, are seeking a deeper life with God. This is something God desires very much—even more than we desire it. While everything we do is by grace—God's power at work in our lives—we must also cooperate with grace through our actions. God will not do it for us. We must act. And that is what you are doing: intentionally creating space for God through reading, study, and reflection. And that is where this journal comes in.

I have kept a journal for decades, and it is a sacred practice for me. As I open myself to God through reading and reflection, I find the Spirit moving in my heart and mind, and my journal is a way to crystalize those thoughts and ideas as a kind of record of my journey with God. I pray that this journal can be that for you as you interact with the Good and Beautiful books.

Grace and peace and joy to you in this journey!

Also from James Bryan Smith

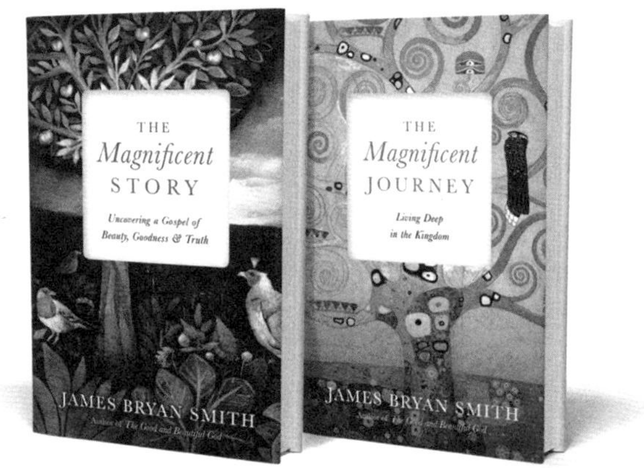